GROSSET & DUNLAP
Penguin Young Readers Group
An Imprint of Penguin Random House LLC

Written by Brandon T. Snider

© 2016 Activision Publishing, Inc. SKYLANDERS, SKYLANDERS SUPERCHARGERS and ACTIVISION are trademarks
of Activision Publishing, Inc. Published by Grosset & Dunlap, an imprint of Penguin Random House LLC, 345 Hudson Street,
New York, New York 10014. GROSSET & DUNLAP is a trademark of Penguin Random House LLC. Printed in the USA.

ISBN 978-0-399-53957-2                                           10 9 8 7 6 5 4 3 2 1

# Portal Master
# Handbook

Grosset & Dunlap
An Imprint of Penguin Random House

# TABLE OF CONTENTS

# WELCOME TO SKYLANDS

Greetings, Portal Master! I am Eon, your guide through this book. Take heed—new and terrible dangers await. You and your Skylanders will need to be prepared for the coming evil, so pay attention to the details contained within this tome, as they will help you on your quest. But first, let me reacquaint you with my wondrous home.

Look to the skies! There you'll find Skylands, an enchanted dimension of floating cloud islands where mysterious elemental energies allow travel to anyplace in the universe.

Each magical island is a completely different world with its own unique identity. Places such as the Pirate Seas, Dragon's Peak, and the Empire of Ice are each filled with incredible and curious power. But these extraordinary energies don't last forever.

On the Cloudbreak Islands, a special volcano erupts once every hundred years, revitalizing Skylands' magical forces.

As a Portal Master and wielder of magic, I've always protected Skylands to the best of my abilities. But even a wise and powerful being like me needs a little help on occasion. The responsibility of keeping this realm safe was far too big to tackle alone, so I gathered a team of heroes from across Skylands to help me.

My Elemental champions, known as the Skylanders, possess amazing powers that they use to help guard the brilliant Core of Light, a device that keeps dark forces at bay.

# MASTER EON & THE SKYLANDERS

As a veteran Portal Master, I know a thing or two about preserving the balance between good and evil. Not only do I command respect among my peers, I quite enjoy drafting bright young heroes into the Skylanders and guiding them on their missions. But while most Portal Masters, like myself, choose a heroic path, not all of them have good intentions.

# KAOS RETURNS

Kaos is a Dark Portal Master who continues to come up with plan after plan to take over Skylands. Some say this is to fulfill his ambition to become Skylands' ultimate evil overlord, though others think that he's still trying to impress his immensely powerful and overbearing mother—herself a Dark Portal Master. Kaos will do whatever it takes to win and should never be underestimated!

Though Kaos has been imprisoned, you can't keep a good bad guy down for long. He just keeps popping his evil head right back up. This time around, the stakes are higher than ever before. Now Kaos has created a device that could very well wipe Skylands off the map!

The Sky Eater is Kaos's brand-new Doomstation of Ultimate Doomstruction. This monstrous new weapon can easily tear through the sky, consuming everything in its path and leaving behind highly unstable rifts that threaten to swallow Skylands whole. The Sky Eater is fueled by a primeval force known as The Darkness.

# SUPERCHARGERS

In order to combat Kaos and The Darkness, the Skylanders sought out the Rift Engines, which were used by the Ancients to explore Skylands and beyond.

Once these powerful artifacts were reclaimed, I selected a unique group of Skylanders and formed an elite strike force—the SuperChargers!

The SuperChargers are able to travel among worlds with relative ease, thanks to their fleet of advanced, Rift Engine-powered vehicles, which greatly enhanced their abilities.

But tragedy soon struck: I was unfortunately captured, and Kaos used his deadly Sky Eater to plunge Skylands into eternal night. Now the Skylanders SuperChargers must rise and challenge Kaos, to ensure the continued existence of Skylands!

# SKYLANDERS ACADEMY

Ending Kaos's reign of terror can take a lot of energy. When the heroes of Skylands need to recharge, they do so at their home base: the prestigious Skylanders Academy. Here they enjoy all the comforts of home while training for their next top secret assignment! Skylanders Academy is filled with an assortment of special rooms and activities to keep the Skylanders busy and entertained.

The three vehicle-training areas are for mastering their combat-driving skills. Don't forget to pick up a Gearbit while you're there!

Pop into the Academy Store to see what new items Ari has for purchase. There are many to choose from.

Persephone the fairy is back. She'll grant your Skylanders upgrades when they gather enough gold!

Enjoy some downtime with friends and play Skystones Overdrive in the Games Room. You can also listen to excerpts from Kaos's diaries while you're there.

You'll get a random collectible when you throw a Wish Stone into the Wishing Well.

Several Skylands Academy residents offer bonus adventures to enterprising Portal Masters. Be sure to pay visits to Tessa, Pandergast, Hugo, and the Great Grizzo!

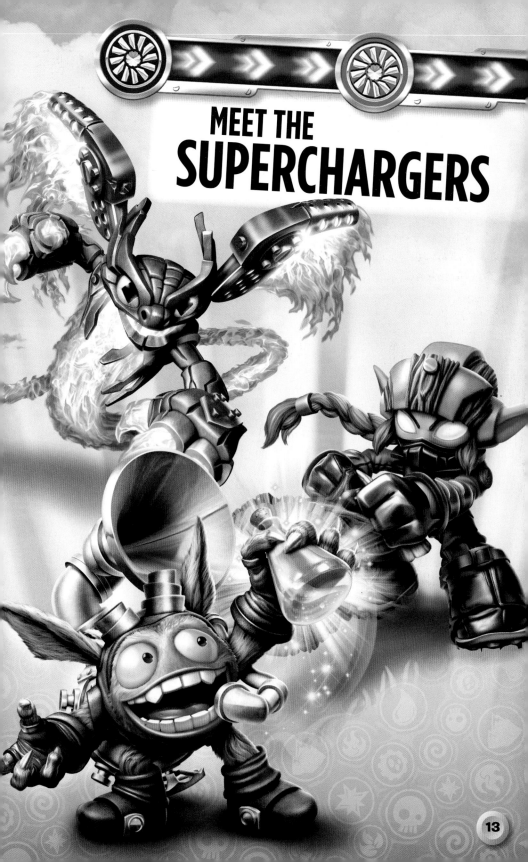

# MEET THE
# SUPERCHARGERS

# SPITFIRE

## "FUEL THE FIRE!"

## STARTING STATS

| | |
|---|---:|
| Max Health | 200 |
| Armor | 18 |
| Speed | 50 |
| Critical Hit | 8 |
| Elemental Power | 25 |

## ORIGIN:

Spitfire doesn't just drive fast—he blazes past his enemies and leaves them smoldering! He's pretty much the best tech-enhanced flame spirit in the entire Skylands Racing Circuit. Some nasty little goblin racer tried to off him during a race through Skywinder Canyon, but Spitfire came back stronger than ever. And when Kaos returned with his Sky Eater, I chose Spitfire to be the leader of my new elite driving team—the SuperChargers!

## PERSONALITY:

He might be unbeatable, but Spitfire is no hothead. His bravery, determination, and tenacity make him a fiery force to be reckoned with.

**SOUL** GEM

**THE FLAMENADOING** Every good Flamenado should begin with a BIG explosion!

# POWERS AND UPGRADES

## ATTACK 1

**BUTANE BRAWLING** Flaming melee combos are blazing the bad guys!

## ATTACK 2

**FLASH FIRE** Bolt forward in an explosive FLASH!

## POWER UPGRADES

### 500 GOLD

**FLAMENADO** Spin around to create a flaming whirlwind!

### 900 GOLD

**FLAME FURY** Charge up! Then run back and forth to strike your foes.

### 700 GOLD

**FLAMENADO CHASERS** Flaming tornadoes will find your enemies and light 'em up!

### 1200 GOLD

**INTENSIFIED FURY** Use a flaming spin attack to boost your melee combo!

---

## "CHOOSE YOUR PATH" UPGRADES

### Path 1: Speed Demon Burn through enemies like a spirited Skylander.

**1700 GOLD**

**MEGA MARATHON** Grow your power, then release! You'll dart around Skylands and take out your enemies.

**2200 GOLD**

**NITRO BOOST** When you're feeling charged, you'll be able to move superfast and avoid damage.

**3000 GOLD**

**TRIATHLETE** How about a couple quick dashes around the world? GO FOR IT!

### Path 2: Fusion Combine the power of the storm and the heat of a torch to become unstoppable!

**1700 GOLD**

**FLAMENADO 2** Turn up the heat with TWO FLAMENADOES!

**2200 GOLD**

**FUEL-INJECTED CLAWS** Draw power from Flamenadoes! Let them superheat your core so you can cause EXTREME DAMAGE.

**3000 GOLD**

**VOLCANIC ARMOR** Don a suit of durable lava armor for added protection.

# SMASH HIT

## "LET'S ROCK!"

## STARTING STATS

| | |
|---|---|
| Max Health | 350 |
| Armor | 24 |
| Speed | 35 |
| Critical Hit | 2 |
| Elemental Power | 25 |

### ORIGIN:

Smash Hit comes from a family of Warsupials whose job it was to clobber dangerous artifacts left over from the Arkeyan Empire. If there's one thing Smash Hit knows, it's how to use his wrecking ball! He's awesome at smashing stuff to bits. He happens to be a pretty skilled fighter as well. That's why I enlisted him into my new crew of SuperChargers.

### PERSONALITY:

Work hard? Smash Hit doesn't know how to do anything else! He's thorough and determined to do the best job he possibly can. *Quitting* isn't in his vocabulary.

## SOUL GEM

**DOWN, UNDER** Generate a big blast underneath you!

# POWERS AND UPGRADES

## STARTING POWERS

### ATTACK 1

**DEMOLISHER** Swing your boulder 'round and 'round!

### ATTACK 2

**CRUSHINATOR** Whack that boulder to pieces.

### 500 GOLD

**CONNECT AND DISCONNECT** Exclusive chain attacks are waiting for you. Go get 'em!

### 700 GOLD

**JUNKYARD DOG** It's a barrage of boulders!

### 900 GOLD

**SPIKEY SPINNER** Charge up and send your boulder spinning.

### 1200 GOLD

**JUNKER** Link up to gain the perfect chain attack.

## "CHOOSE YOUR PATH" UPGRADES

### Path 1: Bolder Boulder Power is in the eye of the boulder.

#### 1700 GOLD

**HEAP** Charge your boulder then release it for maximum destruction!

#### 2200 GOLD

**BETTER TOGETHER** Armor up for added protection.

#### 3000 GOLD

**CATCH!** Toss boulders at your opponents and watch them run!

### Path 2: Chain Champ Behold the chain of command.

#### 1700 GOLD

**G'DAY!** Heave yourself toward an enemy!

#### 2200 GOLD

**CUT LOOSE** Deal your enemy a critical blow.

#### 3000 GOLD

**EARTH CURRENTS** Drag bad guys into the spinning boulder.

# STORMBLADE

## "FEATHER THE STORM!"

### STARTING STATS

| | |
|---|---:|
| Max Health | 220 |
| Armor | 6 |
| Speed | 50 |
| Critical Hit | 6 |
| Elemental Power | 25 |

## ORIGIN:

Ever since she was a kid, Stormblade dreamed of realms beyond her home. When she grew up, she even built a ship called the Sky Slicer so she could race to the edge of the world. She had to know where Skylands ended! I took careful note of Stormblade's passion, and soon gave her a unique role in the SuperChargers that would take her through many undiscovered territories.

## PERSONALITY:

Deep within Stormblade beats the heart and soul of an explorer. Her curiosity is never-ending, just like her supply of positive energy.

### SOUL GEM

**FEATHER WEATHER** Storms of swords shall rain down upon your opponents.

# POWERS AND UPGRADES

## STARTING POWERS

### ATTACK 1

**FEATHER BLADE THROW** Fling that feathered blade!

### ATTACK 2

**STEELED WINDS** Twirl, dash, and damage your enemy. Repeat.

### 500 GOLD

**CYCLONE SURGE** Leap into the sky before you attack.

### 900 GOLD

**FAN OF FEATHERS** Toss a feather spread at a bad guy!

### 700 GOLD

**STORM DIVE** Assault your adversaries from above!

### 1200 GOLD

**FEATHER BARRAGE** Get charged up and release a fusillade of feathers!

## "CHOOSE YOUR PATH" UPGRADES

### Path 1: Wind Warrior The power of wind compels you!

#### 1700 GOLD

**WIND WALL** Destroy projectiles with Steeled Winds!

#### 2200 GOLD

**SHARPENED WINDS** Maximum damage guaranteed.

#### 3000 GOLD

**DOWN DRAFT** Enemies get caught in your windy blowback.

### Path 2: Blade Dancer Feather Dance like no one is watching!

#### 1700 GOLD

**FIST FULL OF FEATHERS** Feathers, feathers, and MORE FEATHERS!

#### 2200 GOLD

**STORM SAIS** Upgrade your feathers to Storm Sais and watch them destroy!

#### 3000 GOLD

**FEATHER THE STORM** Ride that hurricane to stop your enemies.

# FIESTA

## "IT'S PARTY TIME!"

## STARTING STATS

| | |
|---|---:|
| Max Health | 230 |
| Armor | 6 |
| Speed | 50 |
| Critical Hit | 4 |
| Elemental Power | 25 |

## SOUL GEM

**FAMILY FIESTA** Call everyone you know. IT'S PARTY TIME.

### ORIGIN:

As the leader of Count Moneybone's personal mariachi band, Fiesta felt like he was on top of the Underworld. Then one day, a group of Skylanders arrived, revealing the count's plan to attack Skylands with a fleet of killer robots. Fiesta felt duped by his boss, and he decided to join forces with the Skylanders to defeat Count Moneybone once and for all. Fiesta's boldness caught my eye, and I recruited him into the SuperChargers.

### PERSONALITY:

Fiesta might be Undead, but he definitely knows how to be the life of the party. He's super-brave, but ever since Count Moneybone's betrayal, his trust must be well-earned.

# POWERS AND UPGRADES

## ATTACK 1

**TRUMPET CONCORD** Play a tune to damage your adversary.

## ATTACK 2

**AMIGOS** Call on your Amigos to help you kick bad-guy butt!

## POWER UPGRADES

### 500 **GOLD**

**LAID LOW** Hide yourself when things get tough.

### 900 **GOLD**

**SOLO** One note is all it takes to win.

### 700 **GOLD**

**MACHO AMIGOS** Amigos are back and packin' more punch!

### 1200 **GOLD**

**ENCORE** Five solo notes in a row will keep your Amigos around longer!

## "CHOOSE YOUR PATH" UPGRADES

### Path 1: What Amigos Are For Friends forever!

#### 1700 **GOLD**

**TAKE IT AWAY, AMIGOS!** Every fifth solo note gives your Amigos a damage boost!

#### 2200 **GOLD**

**MUCHO AMIGOS** Assemble up to FIVE Amigos!

#### 3000 **GOLD**

**SOUL JAM** When you're Laid Low, stuff around you moves faster.

### Path 2: Super Star! Show off the power of performance!

#### 1700 **GOLD**

**DIVA** Five solo notes will put you in the spotlight with more money, food, and experience!

#### 2200 **GOLD**

**SHOT TO THE HEART** Stop an enemy with a single note!

#### 3000 **GOLD**

**BIG FINISH** Lay Low, grow large, and EXPLODE!

# DIVE-CLOPS

## "LOOK OUT BELOW!"

## STARTING STATS

| | |
|---|---|
| Max Health | 250 |
| Armor | 30 |
| Speed | 35 |
| Critical Hit | 4 |
| Elemental Power | 25 |

## ORIGIN:

Poor Dive-Clops. Back when he was a kid hanging out with his twin brother, Eye-Brawl, his batwings were blown off and he plunged into the murky depths of the Swirling Sea. There he was greeted by Jelly Dwarves, who welcomed him into their Corral Castle and presented him with an amazing dive suit. He used that suit to explore the Whirlpool of Destiny in the ocean's depths, emerging thousands of years later just in time to help me as a member of the SuperChargers.

## PERSONALITY:

Dive-Clops is a curious type, but a little world-weary due to his early misfortunes. Now that he's out of the water, though, he's got his eye focused on being a hero.

## SOUL GEM

**DEPTH OF FIELD** Fire up a barrage of Waterpedoes and lots of mini Waterpedoes.

# POWERS AND UPGRADES

## STARTING POWERS

### ATTACK 1

**WATERPEDO** Watch your Waterpedo explode when it's hit with Sonar!

### ATTACK 2

**SONAR** Damage your enemies with a well-placed Sonar sting!

### 500 GOLD

**PUT THE EYE IN GEYSER** Blast bad guys with a gushing Geyser!

### 900 GOLD

**POWER OF THE PUPIL** While using Geyser, try a special attack.

### 700 GOLD

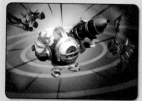

**ECHO ENHANCER** Use Sonar to push back enemies and beat 'em up!

### 1200 GOLD

**PING** Find your target and turn your torpedoes loose!

## "CHOOSE YOUR PATH" UPGRADES

### Path 1: Tidal Torpedoes Use lost deep-sea technology to increase your power!

#### 1700 GOLD

**TORPESLOW** Homing Waterpedoes will seek and slow your enemy.

#### 2200 GOLD

**MARK II WATERPEDO** A couple of Waterpedoes circle their target before blasting it.

#### 3000 GOLD

**NEATO WATERPEDO** Every other Waterpedo is SUPER and does lots of damage in a big area.

### Path 2: Dousing Dowser Study your Sonar capabilities and defeat evil once and for all.

#### 1700 GOLD

**SONAR SMARTS** Sonar attacks damage enemies who are weakened by Waterpedoes.

#### 2200 GOLD

**COUNTER MEASURES** Release a small Sonar pulse when hit by your opponent.

#### 3000 GOLD

**HATCH OFF TO YOU** Use your Geyser for as long as it takes to win!

TECH

# HIGH VOLT

## "PROTECT AND SURGE!"

## STARTING STATS

| | |
|---|---|
| Max Health | 260 |
| Armor | 24 |
| Speed | 50 |
| Critical Hit | 2 |
| Elemental Power | 25 |

## SOUL GEM

**RE-FUSED** Block to restore health.
Live to fight and fight to live!

## ORIGIN:

High Volt was once the commander of an elite security team. He monitored the border where the Skylands meets the Outlands from atop his perch on the Shockspire Tower. He's seen it all—Troll assaults, Greeble invasions, you name it! But when he discovered Kaos was building his Doom Station of Ultimate Doomstruction, High Volt did the right thing and warned me about the growing evil. I eagerly welcomed him into the ranks of the Skylanders SuperChargers in an effort to stop Kaos once and for all.

## PERSONALITY:

High Volt is devoted to his leadership duties. He's always keeping an eye out for trouble. He's also very protective of his friends and does whatever it takes to help them.

# POWERS AND UPGRADES

## ATTACK 1

**STATIC SPEAR** Use your Static Spear to scrap with your enemies!

## ATTACK 2

**SHOCK-IT SHIELD** Block attacks and release charges to blast bad guys!

## POWER UPGRADES

### 500 GOLD

**TRAVELING LIGHT** Toss your Static Spear and create a wall of pure electricity!

### 900 GOLD

**INSULATED IRON** How about some powerful new armor?

### 700 GOLD

**QUICK CURRENTS** Move anywhere you want. It's easy!

### 1200 GOLD

**AMPED LAMP** Charge your staff and let it rip!

### Path 1: Light Fighter Zap your attackers with electric energy!

**1700 GOLD**

**BRING INTO LIGHT** Enemies get caught in your electric beam and end up in trouble.

**2200 GOLD**

**STUN SHOCKED** Throw your Static Spear and watch its electric beam damage bad guys.

**3000 GOLD**

**BLACK OUT** Blitz your enemies and increase your critical hit chance.

### Path 2: Light in Shining Armor More electric-beam POWER? Yes, please!

**1700 GOLD**

**BRIGHT IDEA** Toss that Static Spear and do even more damage than before!

**2200 GOLD**

**EVERYTHING IS RELATIVE** Enemies caught in your electric field are now slowed down.

**3000 GOLD**

**UNBREAKABLE** Stay strong and healthy for maximum fighting power!

# SPLAT

## "THE ART OF WAR!"

| STARTING STATS | |
|---|---|
| Max Health | 240 |
| Armor | 6 |
| Speed | 43 |
| Critical Hit | 4 |
| Elemental Power | 25 |

## ORIGIN:

Living in a faun village was totally boring to Splat. Everyone did the same stuff day in and day out! Most of the fauns liked painting portraits of their great ancestor Fluty Hoofdancer—but not Splat. She'd sneak away to practice her free-form fighting skills. When a group of Drow attacked, she defended her village while everyone else ran away frightened. Her warrior spirit caught my eye, earning her a place among the Skylanders SuperChargers.

## PERSONALITY:

Splat is the definition of spunky! She's got a lot of fight in her and rarely backs down from a ruckus. Splat's also known to be quite brave when duty calls.

## SOUL GEM

**BRINGING THE STAIN** Ink attacks will slow your enemies to a crawl.

# POWERS AND UPGRADES

## ATTACK 1

**ARTISAN ARTS** Bash bad guys with your brush staff!

## ATTACK 2

**HEAVE HUE!** Toss an ink bomb and watch it blow!

## POWER UPGRADES

### 500 GOLD

**HAVE AN INKLING** Use your Inkling to nip your enemies.

### 900 GOLD

**BROAD STROKES** Bigger ink blobs explode with force!

### 700 GOLD

**DYE HARD** Melee attacks are the worst. The sparkly bits tickle!

### 1200 GOLD

**SCAPE-GOAT** Three Scape-Goats appear to charge your foes.

## "CHOOSE YOUR PATH" UPGRADES

### Path 1: Prolific Painter Ink pools and ink creatures, oh my!

#### 1700 GOLD

**WET PAINT** Throw a bursting bomb and leave a pool of ink for enemies to step in.

#### 2200 GOLD

**CANVAS THE AREA** Ink pools created by Wet Paint are even BIGGER.

#### 3000 GOLD

**SHADES OF PAIN** Toss an ink bomb to create a feisty Ink Monster who's not having it.

### Path 2: Abstract Designer Grab a brush and doodle your Inklings into more power!

#### 1700 GOLD

**RUNNING COLORS** Inklings really know how to go the distance.

#### 2200 GOLD

**STROKE OF GENIUS** Unattended Inklings and ink pools now EXPLODE. Watch out!

#### 3000 GOLD

**GRAFFITI GRUFF** Summon a huge Inkling to trample bad guys into dust.

# THRILLIPEDE

## "ALL HANDS ON DECK!"

## STARTING STATS

| | |
|---|---|
| Max Health | 250 |
| Armor | 12 |
| Speed | 50 |
| Critical Hit | 8 |
| Elemental Power | 25 |

### SOUL GEM

**BEAUTIFLIES** Sticky Grenades release healing butterflies. Grab one and use it!

### ORIGIN:

Thrillipede began his career serving as the number one pilot in the Millipede Military. He blasted Greebles out of the sky like crazy! After the Great Greeble War, he returned to his home in Flutter Bay a hero. Captain Flynn at the Skylanders Academy caught wind of Thrillipede's heroic exploits and challenged him to a series of aerial challenges. Thrillipede handily won and soon joined my new team of SuperChargers.

### PERSONALITY:

Thrillipede flies fearlessly through the skies, zipping through the air without a care. He's committed to his duty, but freely admits he loves to wow the crowds.

# POWERS AND UPGRADES

## STARTING POWERS

### ATTACK 1

**BUG BOMB** Look out for that cocoon grenade!

### ATTACK 2

**BEETLE BEATIN'** Swing those arms and strike those baddies!

### 500 GOLD

**COCOONED** Wrap yourself up in a protective cocoon so no one can get you.

### 700 GOLD

**BUG 'N' COVER** Toss a grenade that surrounds your enemies with bugs, slowing them down.

### 900 GOLD

**MIND YOUR BEESWAX** Plant four sticky grenades that explode when bad guys step on them.

### 1200 GOLD

**COCOOTIES** Cover yourself in a cocoon then burst free to damage your enemies!

## "CHOOSE YOUR PATH" UPGRADES

### Path 1: Mighty-Morphosis Transform into a flying fighting machine!

#### 1700 GOLD

**BETTER FLY** Emerge from your cocoon with wings! Bombard enemies with Bug Bombs for maximum damage.

#### 2200 GOLD

**BUGGING OUT** Increase damage by using ALL your grenade projectiles.

#### 3000 GOLD

**TICK IT TO 'EM** Jump up and toss sticky grenades below you!

### Path 2: Insistent Insect Use a swarm of insects to overwhelm your enemies!

#### 1700 GOLD

**GNAWING GNATS** Bug Bombs are filled with tiny insects that eat their enemies and slowly damage them over time.

#### 2200 GOLD

**NESTING GNATS** Swarming insects stack up to five times and do double the damage!

#### 3000 GOLD

**INSECT EPIDEMIC** Bad guys who've been swarmed by too many insects EXPLODE.

LIGHT

# ASTROBLAST

## "READY, SET, GLOW!"

### STARTING STATS

| | |
|---|---|
| Max Health | 180 |
| Armor | 18 |
| Speed | 35 |
| Critical Hit | 6 |
| Elemental Power | 25 |

### ORIGIN:

Astroblast was on a top secret mission when he crashed his ship, the Sun Runner, on a desolate island. There he encountered an ancient Rift Engine, a relic that served as a Portal between worlds. Then a battalion of evil Trolls tried to steal it from him! After a fierce laser battle, the Trolls fled in defeat. Later, I appeared before Astroblast in my holographic form and thanked him for his great service. Fortunately, I was able to convince him to return the Rift Engine to Skylanders Academy and join my new team of SuperChargers.

### SOUL GEM

**WOOL ENCOUNTERS** Summon a space rock containing a creature with a laser gun who's ready to BLAAAAST!

### PERSONALITY:

Astroblast is a curious type who won't back down from a fight. He's always prepared to protect people (and relics like the Rift Engines) from danger.

# POWERS AND UPGRADES

### ATTACK 1

**SOLAR FLAIR** Fire beams of condensed sunlight and watch them bounce around!

### ATTACK 2

**ASTEROID BELT** Toss a prismatic space rock and watch its dust slow down your enemies.

## POWER UPGRADES

### 500 GOLD

**STARSAULT** Knock back bad guys with a swift kick!

### 700 GOLD

**SOLAR FIELD** Fast-moving light particles power up your armor and protect you from harm. Life Skylanders nearby also regenerate your health!

### 900 GOLD

**SOLAR POWERED** The Solar Flair laser has the power of a hundred suns!

### 1200 GOLD

**SPACE ROCKS!** Summon a space rock down upon the head of your worst enemy.

### Path 1: Cosmic Technology Power up your gear to gain new laser abilities!

#### 1700 GOLD

**SURFACE OF THE SUN** Heat up your Solar Flair and watch bad guys feel the burn.

#### 2200 GOLD

**MEATIER METEORS** Bring down a GIANT space rock on an opponent's head.

#### 3000 GOLD

**STAR LIGHT, STAR BRIGHT** When in doubt, blast 'em with Solar Flairs.

### Path 2: Nova Hopper Hallelujah! It's raining space rocks!

#### 1700 GOLD

**METEOR SHOWER** Launch a bunch of meteors at one time.

#### 2200 GOLD

**FULL SPECTRUM** Your space rock's dust trail is THICK. Shoot your Solar Flair into it and create a light show to distract your enemies.

#### 3000 GOLD

**SUPERNOVA** You've got one chance! Go SUPERNOVA and gain back half your health.

# NIGHTFALL

## "DARK AND DANGEROUS!"

## STARTING STATS

| | |
|---|---|
| Max Health | 230 |
| Armor | 6 |
| Speed | 43 |
| Critical Hit | 10 |
| Elemental Power | 25 |

## ORIGIN:

Nightfall hated being bored. She loved to leave the poison clouds of Fogshadow Tower to go exploring outside the Poison Sea. Her other Dreadwalker friends dared not leave their homes, but she preferred to search the deepest underwater caverns, protected by the Sea Shadow, her submarine. When a gigantic sea monster reared its ugly head, Nightfall blasted it and saved her people. I was impressed by her bravery and drafted her into my legendary team of SuperChargers.

## PERSONALITY:

Nightfall is inquisitive and energetic, and loves exploring. She cares deeply for her people, but has never cared about being popular or fitting in with the crowd.

## SOUL GEM

**BAD HAIR DAY** Corral bad guys into an area with Whip Lash, then knock them all down in one fell swoop.

# POWERS AND UPGRADES

### ATTACK 1

**HANDY HOOKS** Attack your enemy with a barrage of right and left hooks!

### ATTACK 2

**AMBRUSH** Dart in front of or behind bad guys.

## POWER UPGRADES

### 500 **GOLD**

**WHIP LASH** Use a lock of hair to whip opponents into the air and then knock them down!

### 900 **GOLD**

**HAIR TODAY, GONE NOW** Weaken enemies during Ambrush and move FAST.

### 700 **GOLD**

**SPLIT HOOK ENDS** New hooks cause melee attacks to do A LOT of damage.

### 1200 **GOLD**

**LAYERED LUNGE** The first hook melee attack after Ambrush is a critical strike!

## Path 1: Master Angler Learn to swing those super-sharp hooks.

### 1700 **GOLD**

**SPLITTING HAIRS** Unleash a crazy combo attack of hooks and hair!

### 2200 **GOLD**

**COMB-O** Every fourth attack sends your enemies to their doom!

### 3000 **GOLD**

**PLAYING HOOKY** You'll be dealin' out the damage when you're in a large area.

## Path 2: Dread Head Master the use of your dark energy attacks.

### 1700 **GOLD**

**AMBRUSH RUSH** Shoot strands of hair at bad guys who stand in your way.

### 2200 **GOLD**

**UP-SWEEP** Blast your enemies into the air!

### 3000 **GOLD**

**VAST VOLUME** Use three strands of hair to send enemies into the air during Whip Lash.

# RETURNING HEROES

I invited some of my most reliable and dedicated Skylanders to join the SuperChargers, as well. These veterans have proven that they can stand up to the worst of Kaos's minions in battle. Of course, we wouldn't send them back out to fight without a few upgrades!

## Lava Lance Eruptor

### "BORN TO BURN!"

This fiery fury returns with a new suit of armor, and a sharp lance made out of—you guessed it—lava! Eruptor has learned some new tricks, both in and out of his vehicle, the Burn-Cycle. Try out his upgrades to improve lancing abilities and make volcanoes and eruptions, too.

### STARTING STATS

| Max Health | 290 | Speed | 35 | Elemental | |
|---|---|---|---|---|---|
| Armor | 24 | Critical Hit | 8 | Power | 25 |

## Shark Shooter Terrafin

### "IT'S FEEDING TIME!"

The toughest dirt shark in Skylands just got even tougher! In addition to swimming and slamming, he's now equipped with a shark rocket launcher, which is just as amazing as it sounds. Upgrade Terrafin to help him and his new miniature allies wreak havoc on minions from beneath the ground!

### STARTING STATS

| Max Health | 270 | Speed | 35 | Elemental | |
|---|---|---|---|---|---|
| Armor | 24 | Critical Hit | 4 | Power | 25 |

# Hurricane Jet-Vac

## "HAWK AND AWE!"

Jet-Vac has always harnessed the power of the Air Element in creative ways, and his new Jet Turbine Vacuum is no exception! His new contraption shoots fan blades that can bounce off multiple enemies, and his new upgraded wind power leaves furious hurricanes in his wake!

### STARTING STATS

| | | | | | |
|---|---|---|---|---|---|
| Max Health | 240 | Speed | 43 | Elemental | |
| Armor | 12 | Critical Hit | 6 | Power | 25 |

# Bone Bash
# Roller Brawl

## "LET'S ROLL!"

Just because Roller Brawl's new bone armor hides her vampire fangs doesn't mean she won't use them! This fierce roller-derby jammer demolishes enemies up close and from a distance with her lethal combination of speed, cunning, and—of course—Boomerang Fang Blades.

### STARTING STATS

| | | | | | |
|---|---|---|---|---|---|
| Max Health | 220 | Speed | 50 | Elemental | |
| Armor | 12 | Critical Hit | 6 | Power | 25 |

# Deep Dive Gill Grunt

## "FEAR THE FISH!"

Gill Grunt has exchanged his trusty harpoon for a weapon worthy of the deepest seas—a trident! His enemies may swim away in fear of its pointy end, but Gill Grunt's long-range lightning attack will surely find them in the end. Upgrade Gill Grunt to summon massive sea storms and ride giant waves!

## STARTING STATS

| Max Health | 270 | Speed | 35 | Elemental | |
|---|---|---|---|---|---|
| Armor | 24 | Critical Hit | 6 | Power | 25 |

# Double Dare Trigger Happy

## "NO GOLD, NO GLORY!"

This loose cannon now has a literal cannon at his command. But Trigger Happy isn't shooting cannonballs—he is the cannonball! His tricks aren't just for show, though. These firecrackers and flaming hoops will deal heavy damage to enemies while they're distracted by the spectacle.

## STARTING STATS

| Max Health | 300 | Speed | 50 | Elemental | |
|---|---|---|---|---|---|
| Armor | 18 | Critical Hit | 6 | Power | 25 |

# Big Bubble Pop Fizz

## "MOTION OF THE POTION!"

What's that on Pop Fizz's back? A massive Bubble Blaster, obviously! He's carried his alchemy to new levels with new potion mixtures, and needed a big contraption to match it. All those chemicals make Pop Fizz a little crazy, but he's at his finest when he transforms into his Bubbling Beast form!

### STARTING STATS

| Max Health | 300 | Speed | 43 | Elemental | |
|---|---|---|---|---|---|
| Armor | 24 | Critical Hit | 4 | Power | 25 |

# Super Shot Stealth Elf

## "SILENT BUT DEADLY!"

Only Stealth Elf could sneak around unseen while carrying such a powerful weapon. Her new Dagger Cannon takes out more enemies than ever before, while her turret makes for a handy distraction when she needs to disappear from sight! And should you forget about Stealth Elf's ninja abilities, she'll quickly remind you with her upgraded spin attacks.

### STARTING STATS

| Max Health | 190 | Speed | 50 | Elemental | |
|---|---|---|---|---|---|
| Armor | 12 | Critical Hit | 6 | Power | 25 |

# VEHICLES OF LAND, SEA, AND SKY

FIRE

LAND

DRIVER

SPITFIRE

# HOT STREAK

Hot Streak is Spitfire's custom race car. It was made from elemental magma and forged in the depths of the Volcanic Vault. With maximum firepower, it is capable of achieving extreme speeds and is ready to scorch anything in its path!

**STARTING** ABILITIES

**Performance: Blue-Fire Tires**          Horn: **Searing Snarler**
**Specialty: Blaze Boosters**

**WEAPONS**

**Fire Grill:** Shoot flame at nearby enemies

**Nitro Blaze:** Boost forward in a blaze of flames

# THUMP TRUCK

Thump Truck is Smash Hit's personal wrecking machine that was built for one purpose—total destruction! It has been heavily modified with earth-crunching iron jaws, a gravel exhaust port, and armored steel plating for ultimate toughness!

EARTH

LAND

DRIVER

SMASH HIT

**STARTING** ABILITIES

**Performance: Concrete Chewer**       **Horn: Mammoth Toot**
**Specialty: Fusion Mixer**

**WEAPONS**

**Under Punch:** Uppercut enemies with a giant Earth fist
**Bush Booster:** Gain a speed boost and damaging ram attack

# SKY SLICER

The Sky Slicer is aerodynamic and lightning fast! Originally designed by Stormblade to explore the farthest reaches of Skylands, it has since been retrofitted with high-powered weaponry and armor, making it one of the best in the nest!

**STARTING** ABILITIES

| | |
|---|---|
| Performance: **Katar Wing** | Horn: **Cloud** |
| Specialty: **Screamstream Thrust** | **Reverberator** |

**WEAPONS**

**Feather Fury:** Shoot out feathered spears
**Pigeon Flock Missiles:** Shoot out lots of homing missiles

# CRYPT CRUSHER

The Crypt Crusher is the undefeated champion of Underworld drag racing. Originally crafted from Fiesta's childhood race-car bed, it now uses an intimidating Wheel of Doom to roll over the competition!

## STARTING ABILITIES

**Performance: Coffin Clapper**
**Specialty: Grave Raiser**

**Horn: Decomposition**

## WEAPONS

**Tune Up:** Shoot homing notes at enemies
**Amigo Amplitude:** Shoot Amigos that attach to enemies and cause damage over time. Keeping Amigos on the Crypt Crusher will power up the Tune Up weapon.

# DIVE BOMBER

The Dive Bomber is a heavy-duty aquatic battle tank! With enchanted metal plating capable of withstanding the immense pressure of the deep ocean, evil has nowhere to hide when Dive-Clops is in pursuit!

**STARTING** ABILITIES

Performance: **Torpedo Buoys**          Horn: **Dolphin Disorienter**
Specialty: **Power Propellor**

**WEAPONS**

**Twin Torpedo Tubes:** Shoot torpedoes at enemies
**Deep Sea Sonar:** Damage nearby enemies and mark targets for homing torpedoes

# SHIELD STRIKER

TECH

LAND

DRIVER

HIGH VOLT

The Shield Striker is the ultimate weapon against evil. Heavily armored and surging with electricity, High Volt's high-powered machine is geared up to enforce justice on anything that stands in its way!

**STARTING** ABILITIES

Performance: **Troll Patroller**          Horn: **Redirector**
Specialty: **Tactical Viewer**

**WEAPONS**

**Crowd Control:** Shoot nearby enemies with electricity
**Doomproof Forcefield:** Absorb attack damage with shield, then release to explode the shield, dealing increased damage

# SPLATTER SPLASHER

The Splatter Splasher is a high-speed hydro-craft that leaves evil floating in its wake! With its ultraslick armor and underwater enchantment, Splat's custom ride is a force to be reckoned with above and below the surface!

## STARTING ABILITIES

**Performance: Easel Exhausts**          **Horn: Bristle Whistle**
**Specialty: Speed Sculpture**

## WEAPONS

**Oiled Ink:** Shoot ink at enemies in front of you
**Inkling Interceptor:** Lay down an Inkling that attacks nearby enemies

# BUZZ WING

LIFE

SKY

DRIVER

THRILLIPEDE

Buzz Wing is Thrillipede's famous fighter plane. After heroically blasting over three hundred enemy jets in the Great Greeble War, it was put on display in the Millipede Museum. But with Kaos on the loose again, it's back in action and ready for more!

**STARTING** ABILITIES

Performance: **Monarch Lifters**          Horn: **Cricket Crackler**
Specialty: **Butterfly Flappers**

**WEAPONS**

**Insect Swarmer:** Shoot a blast of insects at enemies in front of you
**Swarm Trail:** Get a speed boost and leave a swarm of damaging butterflies in your wake

# SUN RUNNER

The Sun Runner is a prototype spaceship built to recover items that are lost when traveling through the Portals. Its antigravity capabilities and speedy acceleration allow Astroblast to get the jump on bad guys before they know what hit them!

**STARTING** ABILITIES

**Performance: Star Crystals**　　　**Horn: Noisy Nebulizer**
**Specialty: Shuttle Dome**

**WEAPONS**

**Light-Matter Laser:** Shoot lasers at enemies
**Satellite Support:** Call for a large laser to shoot down at enemies

# SEA SHADOW

The Sea Shadow was originally built by Nightfall to explore the shadowy depths of the Poison Sea near her home. It is elusive and agile, with powerful weaponry that will sting any monster that lurks in the abyss!

**STARTING** ABILITIES

Performance: **Sea Chasm Turbine**
Specialty: **Undercurrent Catcher**

Horn: **Night Time Tuner**

**WEAPONS**

**Abyss Cannon:** Shoot orbs of Darkness at enemies in front of you, or a Luminescent Orb for a huge explosion

**Luminescent Launcher:** Shoot a Luminescent Orb forward, highlighting an area where Abyssal Orbs will do more damage

FIRE

LAND

DRIVER
LAVA LANCE ERUPTOR

# BURN-CYCLE

The Burn-Cycle was created when Eruptor attempted to roll hot lava into a "flaming snowman" during the Skylander holiday party. The result was a perpetual fireball with incredibly high acceleration and blurring speeds!

**STARTING** ABILITIES

**Performance: Cracked Core Fender**
**Specialty: Molten Boosters**

**Horn: Eruption**
**Uproar**

**WEAPONS**

**Delayed Blast Pyreball:** Shoot a sticky pyreball that explodes on enemies

**Releasing Fire:** Lay down a trail of fire behind you

# SHARK TANK

The Shark Tank is an unstoppable driving force when Terrafin is at the helm. Containing subterranean navigation, all-terrain teeth treads, and enchanted battle armor, it is primed and ready to take the *bite* to Kaos!

## STARTING ABILITIES

**Performance: Geode Grinders**          **Horn: Quarry Clang**
**Specialty: Subterrain Glider**

## WEAPONS

**Ballistic Drill Missile:** Shoot a large homing missile
**Street Swimming:** Swim under the road

# JET STREAM

Jet Stream is a finely tuned storm-chasing machine. Its twin turbines give it supreme maneuverability, while its Sky Baron battle armor and enhanced weaponry guarantee it will always be the last bird standing!

## STARTING ABILITIES

**Performance: Wind Slashers**          Horn: **Turbine Trumpet**
**Specialty: Wind Frenzies**

## WEAPONS

**Avian Razors:** Shoot bouncing blades at nearby enemies
**Vacuum Bomb:** Explosive bomb that traps enemies in a vacuum

# TOMB BUGGY

The Tomb Buggy was handcrafted by Roller Brawl from the skeletal remains of an ancient undead Grave Panther. With its agile maneuverability and impressive weaponry, it's perfect for any driver who has a bone to pick with evil!

**STARTING** ABILITIES

**Performance: Grave Crackers**          **Horn: Scream Screech**
**Specialty: Boo-ster**

**WEAPONS**

**Spread the Love:** Shoot a wave of Undead power at enemies
**Unfair Play:** Create a large beam of energy that damages enemies next to the vehicle

# REEF RIPPER

WATER

SEA

DRIVER

DEEP DIVE GILL GRUNT

The Reef Ripper is the legendary submarine that Gill Grunt uses to scour the vast ocean for his lost love. Armed with a siren blast and a harpoon launcher, it guarantees that the evil pirates that took her won't be getting off the hook very easily!

**STARTING** ABILITIES

Performance: **Gill Grill**          Horn: **Revving Gurgler**
Specialty: **Aqua Fin Turbine**

**WEAPONS**

**Ocean Upheaval:** Shoot a trident at enemies
**Electrify the Tail:** Electrify nearby enemies

# GOLD RUSHER

The Gold Rusher is an all-purpose high-performance stunt vehicle. Packed with hyper-powered exhaust pipes and leprechaun-gold plating, Trigger Happy's custom ride is the flashiest vehicle in the SuperCharger fleet!

**STARTING** ABILITIES

**Performance: Pop & Sparkers**          **Horn: Clink Clankers**
**Specialty: Cogwheel Trike**

**WEAPONS**

**Currency Cannon:** Rapidly shoot coins at nearby enemies

**Triggered Happy Mines:** Lay down huge mines that explode when enemies touch them

# SODA SKIMMER

The Soda Skimmer is a rip-roaring, rapid-riding machine! Running entirely on jet-potion and built with an indestructible inflatable material called "Bafloon" (created by Pop Fizz himself), this vehicle has all the right ingredients!

## STARTING ABILITIES

**Performance: Gushing Geysers**  **Horn: Pressure Blare**
**Specialty: Inner Beast Tube**

## WEAPONS

**Alchemic Admixture:** Shoot a custom potion mixture at enemies in front of you
**Shake and Change:** Mix potions to change the shot type for Alchemic Admixture, damaging nearby enemies as you mix

# STEALTH STINGER

The Stealth Stinger is the ultimate forest ninja weapon! During covert Skylander operations, Stealth Elf uses its camouflage abilities and high-velocity thorn rockets to sneak past enemies and get the drop on evil!

LIFE

SKY

DRIVER

SUPER SHOT STEALTH ELF

**STARTING** ABILITIES

Performance: **Leaf Cutters**          Horn: **Woodland Tune**
Specialty: **Waxed Wood Plates**

**WEAPONS**

**Canopy Piercer:** Shoot acorn bullets at enemies
**Forest Fog:** Disappear in a cloud of forest fog for a few seconds

# INTO THE
# ADVENTURE

# THE RIFT TO SKYLANDS

**K**aos has seized complete control over the Portal network which leads into Skylands! Flynn, Cali, and Hugo are being held on a prison transport ship. Use your SuperCharged vehicle to enter the Portal network to rescue your friends before all of the entrances to the Skylands collapse—forever.

## GOAL
- Reach Skylands

## QUESTS
- Distress Call
- The Great Escape
- Save the Pit Crew
- Get Back to the Fleet

## COLLECTIONS
- 5 Epic Treasure Chests

Make sure you collect all three sparks to gain additional Stardust when you finish a lock-picking puzzle. You'll increase your Portal Master Rank!

Keep your eyes peeled for Red Toolboxes as you complete Land, Sea, and Sky segments. These Toolboxes contain modifications for your SuperCharger's vehicle.

Each Gearbit is worth three instead of one! Collect them by drifting and doing barrel rolls.

# THE CLOUDBREATHER'S CRAG

Hugo possesses the Sock of Eon, a "precious" relic preserved through the ages. If you bring the Sock to the Cloudbreather Dragon, a huge and fabled beast said to be able to sniff out anything at any distance, you may be able to track down Master Eon. However, hundreds of towns and villages around Skylands have fallen under Kaos's diabolical reign . . . including those in the dragon's homelands, the Cloudscraper Mountains.

## GOAL
- Find the Cloudbreather so he can give you a map to locate Eon

## QUESTS
- Talk to the Cloudbreather
- Ring the Dragon Gong
- Destroy the Blockages
- Kite Mini Game: Use the kite to collect coins
- Rescue the Miners
- Destroy Kaos's Fleet
- Save the Temple
- Test Drive

## COLLECTIONS
- 6 Epic Treasure Chests
- 1 SuperCharger Gate

Stop by a vehicle upgrade station and use your hard-earned Gearbits to increase your vehicle's weapons and shields.

Persephone is ready to take your Gold in exchange for access to brand-new capabilities!

Epic Treasure Chests can be hidden in the most unlikely places! Remember to search around, behind, and under things to find these bounty-filled rewards.

# THE CLOUD KINGDOM

Master Eon is being held prisoner in the Land of the Undead by Count Moneybone, but the Rift Engine of your vehicle isn't powerful enough to reach through the cosmic barrier to enter another dimension. You need to harness the incredible energy of the Thunderous Bolt, a magical artifact of the Cloud Kingdom, to upgrade your Rift Engine. Unfortunately, not all is well in the Cloud Kingdom: the pompous Lord Stratosfear has staged a coup and stolen the Bolt for himself.

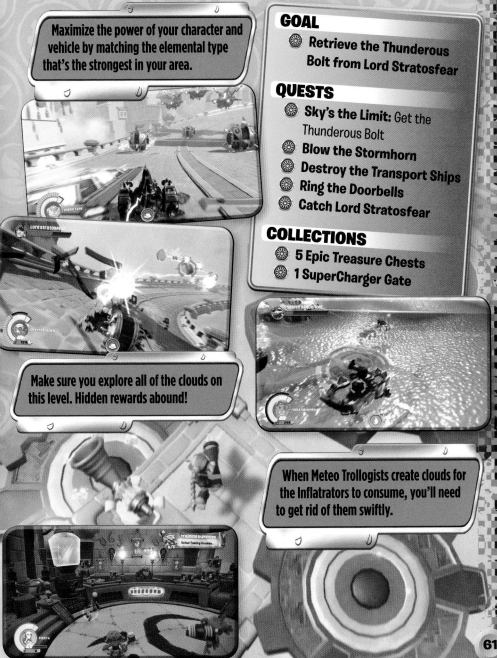

Maximize the power of your character and vehicle by matching the elemental type that's the strongest in your area.

## GOAL

- Retrieve the Thunderous Bolt from Lord Stratosfear

## QUESTS

- **Sky's the Limit:** Get the Thunderous Bolt
- **Blow the Stormhorn**
- **Destroy the Transport Ships**
- **Ring the Doorbells**
- **Catch Lord Stratosfear**

## COLLECTIONS

- 5 Epic Treasure Chests
- 1 SuperCharger Gate

Make sure you explore all of the clouds on this level. Hidden rewards abound!

When Meteo Trollogists create clouds for the Inflatrators to consume, you'll need to get rid of them swiftly.

# LAND OF THE UNDEAD

Supercharged with the power of ten jillion thunderbolts, you can safely enter the Land of the Undead to stage a rescue mission for Master Eon. It's not as easy as just getting there, though. Count Moneybone's Dehabilitation Center is a fiendish maze of mixed-up perspectives, and Master Eon is being held in an impenetrable maximum-security Traptanium cell.

## GOAL
- Use the Thunderous Bolt to overcharge your vehicle, and enter the Land of the Undead to find Eon

## QUESTS
- Rescue Master Eon
- Help Prisoners Escape
- Blow Up the Statue
- Destroy Blockage
- Defeat Moneybone

## COLLECTIONS
- 7 Epic Treasure Chests
- 1 SuperCharger Gate

Avoid ALL green searchlights! If you're spotted by one, you could end up getting bombed—or worse.

Collect all three Sparks to acquire additional Stardust toward your Portal Master Rank.

Be on the lookout for places you can use explosive barrels. You might just uncover some treasure!

# BATTLEBRAWL ISLAND

**M**aster Eon is free, and you have no time to waste. Throughout the ages, many heroes have defeated The Darkness. Their stories have been written down in the Spell Punk Library, but the library is huge (not to mention cursed). You'll need a guide. Luckily, there's a Spell Punk on Battlebrawl Island who's offering one favor to any Skylander who can beat him in a one-on-one fight . . . The only catch is that he's never been defeated.

## GOAL
- Become the champion of Battlebrawl Island, and earn a favor from the current champion, Spellslamzer

## QUESTS
- Get into the Arena
- Defeat Brimstone and Boulders
- Defeat the Pirates
- Defeat Spellslamzer

## COLLECTIONS
- 2 Epic Treasure Chests

To unlock additional Stardust and increase your Portal Master Rank, remember to access your Portal Master Emblems!

**SHANK**
I just so happen to have a flask of "Wake the Dead" ov

Save your health items as much as possible. You're going to need 'em!

Defeat rival Skystones Overdrive players and receive a unique Skystones card.

# THE SPELL PUNK LIBRARY

Spellslamzer guides you to the Hall of the Ancients in the Spell Punk Library. There, you find several ancient and magical tomes which chronicle heroic battles against The Darkness through the ages. There must be some clue about how to defeat The Darkness somewhere in those books . . .

## GOAL
- Learn how to defeat The Darkness by exploring ancient, magical tomes

## QUESTS
- Big Book of Secrets
- **Book 1:** The Darkness
- **Book 2:** Charge of the First Light Squadron
- **Book 3:** The Ancients' Plan
- **Book 4:** The Hydra
- **Book 5:** The Core of Light

## COLLECTIONS
- 6 Epic Treasure Chests
- 1 SuperCharger Gate

If you're having trouble in vehicle sections, just remember to switch your modifications. This will allow you to adapt to each unique situation.

Move furniture around in the Spell Punk Library to reveal hidden Treasure Chests and rewards!

# GADFLY GLADES

The Core of Light seems to be the key to defeating The Darkness, but the only person who knows how to transform the Core from a shield to a weapon is the author of the books you explored: Pomfrey Le Fuzzbottom, a tiny worm who isn't quite as young as he used to be. Pomfrey's plan was to move to a place called Gadfly Glades to work in solitude, but an enthusiastic young collector known as the Troubletaker has put his retirement plans on hold.

Don't step in a Toxic Tushie cloud! It's poisonous and can cause a lot of damage.

## GOAL
- Locate the author of the Darkness books (Pomfrey) and have him tell you how to turn the Core of Light into a weapon

## QUESTS
- Save the Twitterpillars
- Shut Off the Water
- Rescue Pomfrey

## COLLECTIONS
- 6 Epic Treasure Chests
- 1 SuperCharger Gate

Keep an eye out for Cootie Trap attacks. Make sure to dodge them or you'll end up with serious damage.

Persephone knows a lot of good stuff. Make sure you speak with her about spending your coins in exchange for upgrades.

# CAP'N CLUCK'S CHICKEN HQ

Pomfrey tells you that you'll need the Eye of the Ancients to weaponize the Core of Light. To claim the Eye, you'll need to defeat the Titans of the Monstrous Isles—and to fight a Titan, you must become a Titan. Cluck, one of your old enemies, owns an enchanted seed called the Kolossal Kernel, which has the power to supersize anything that it touches. He's using the Kernel's powers to build an army of super-soldiers, as well as an unstoppable fast-food empire. You'll need to infiltrate his secret headquarters to retrieve the Kernel.

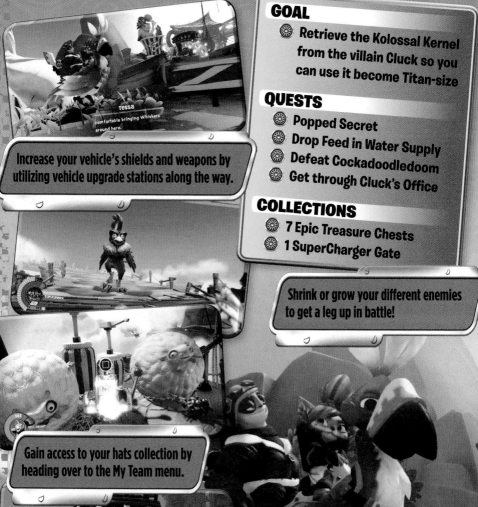

tessa
comfortable bringing Whiskers
around here.

Increase your vehicle's shields and weapons by utilizing vehicle upgrade stations along the way.

## GOAL
- Retrieve the Kolossal Kernel from the villain Cluck so you can use it become Titan-size

## QUESTS
- Popped Secret
- Drop Feed in Water Supply
- Defeat Cockadoodledoom
- Get through Cluck's Office

## COLLECTIONS
- 7 Epic Treasure Chests
- 1 SuperCharger Gate

Shrink or grow your different enemies to get a leg up in battle!

Gain access to your hats collection by heading over to the My Team menu.

# MONSTROUS ISLES

The Darkness realizes that you and your allies have a fighting chance. Kaos and The Darkness rally together—and in the process, Kaos fires Glumshanks. The residents of the Academy take him in as you chow down on the Kolossal Kernel and set out to take on the Titans of the Monstrous Isles.

Smash sand buildings to look for treasure and health items.

## GOAL
- Eat the Kernel and become Titan-size so you can defeat the massive Titans and retrieve the Eye of the Ancients, the last piece needed to weaponize the Core of Light

## QUESTS
- Destroy Clam Bunkers
- Catch Beachcomber
- Destroy Sandcastles

## COLLECTIONS
- 4 Epic Treasure Chests
- 1 SuperCharger Gate

Make sure you finish the Sea Vehicle Segment in order to combat Beachcomber with the greatest amount of power.

The Pterashark is a tough nut to crack! Hit him when he's tired and, when he goes underground, run away. Complete the Sky Vehicle segment to gain maximum advantage.

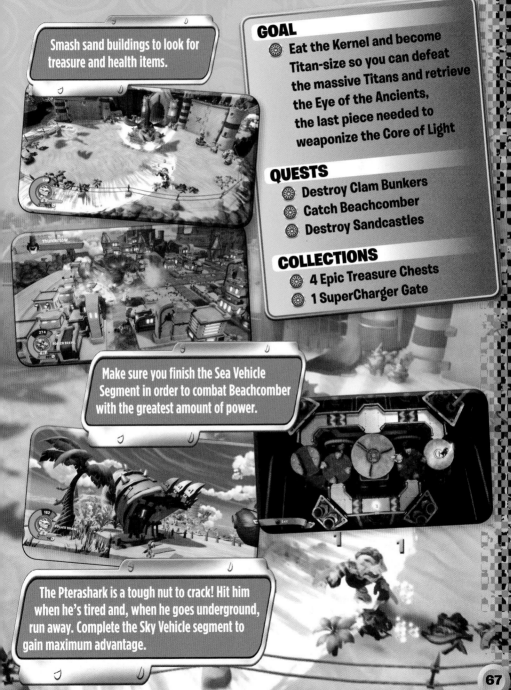

# RIDEPOCALYPSE DEMOLITION DERBY

**K**aos launches an attack on the Skylander Academy. You and your allies narrowly escape thanks to a heroic sacrifice by Glumshanks, but the Core of Light is destroyed, the Academy is badly damaged, and Glumshanks seems lost forever. You soon learn that a huckster named Pandergast has rescued Glumshanks and is offering him as the first-place prize in a seedy demolition derby. You need to save Glumshanks—not just because he knows more about Kaos and the inner workings of the Sky Eater than anyone else in Skylands, but because he saved you.

## GOAL
- Become King Champion Lord of Ridepocalypse, and win Glumshanks back from the dastardly Pandergast

## QUESTS
- Defeat the Enemies

## COLLECTIONS
- 2 Epic Treasure Chests
- 1 SuperCharger Gate

Use your Gearbits at the vehicle upgrade station to increase your shields and weapons. Every upgrade helps!

Each enemy you face in the battle arena has a different weakness. It won't take you long to figure out when you should dodge, when to try and outmaneuver your opponent, and when to strike from behind!

# VAULT OF THE ANCIENTS

It doesn't seem possible to defeat The Darkness without the Core of Light, but you may be able to send it back to where it came from by harnessing the power of the Dark Rift Engine. Glumshanks knows that the Engine is hidden in the Vault of the Ancients, a forbidden place full of cursed magic and terrible traps. It's not an appealing plan . . . but it's your last resort.

## GOAL

- Travel deep through the terrible Vault of the Ancients to find the Dark Rift Engine so you can send The Darkness back to where it came from.

## QUESTS

- Restore Sentry Statues
- Ring the Chimes
- Power the Core

## COLLECTIONS

- 7 Epic Treasure Chests
- 1 SuperCharger Gate

Every enemy responds differently to your Push and Pull power. Use the magnet to gain the upper hand against enemy attacks.

Use the magnet to attract treasure. Be warned! You might attract enemies, as well.

# THE BANDIT TRAIN

The dark magic of the Rift Engine draws unwanted attention to the crippled Academy. Marauding Sky Bandits launch a raid on the Academy and kidnap Mags for her expertise as a mechanic. Without her, your plans are as good as gone. Catch up to the Bandits' runaway Sky Train and sneak in to rescue Mags.

## GOAL

- The Sky Bandits have kidnapped Mags so she'll trick out their train. You need to rescue her.

## QUESTS

- Rescue Mags

## COLLECTIONS

- 4 Epic Treasure Chests
- 1 SuperCharger Gate

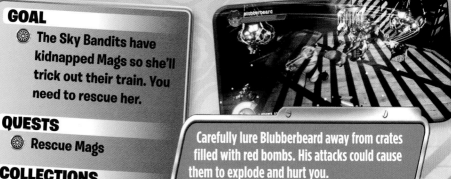

Carefully lure Blubberbeard away from crates filled with red bombs. His attacks could cause them to explode and hurt you.

Watch out! Some crates contain harmful bombs. Make sure you're cautious as you destroy them.

# THE SKY EATER

Thanks to Mags, the work on the Dark Rift Engine is complete. You must transport the Engine into the Sky Eater, and then find your way to Kaos's throne room. It's time to make your final stand before all of Skylands is lost forever.

## GOAL
- Enter the terrifying Sky Eater, and defeat Kaos in single combat

## QUESTS
- Infiltrate Sky Eater
- Get Past Kaos's Defenses
- Hunt and Destroy the Hydra

## COLLECTIONS
- 4 Epic Treasure Chests
- 1 SuperCharger Gate

When fighting a big group of bad guys, make sure you take out the Green Spell Punk first! That way he won't heal the bad guys that you're trying to destroy.

Stepping on the wrong tile can hurt you. Memorize the patterns when the red tiles turn white on the computer. This will indicate a safer path for you to take.

Keep an eye out as you travel through Skylands! There are all sorts of interesting collectible items to gather along the way. Here are some of the things you might encounter.

# Hats

Hats aren't just for looks (though I think they're quite fashionable)! These head-toppers will boost your Skylander's stats as well as give him or her a classy new style.

| Hat | Stats |
|-----|-------|
| Burn-Cycle Header | +7% Critical Hit, +25 Elemental Power |
| Buzz Wing Hat | +15% Critical Hit, +4 Speed, +10 Elemental Power |
| Crypt Crusher Cap | +30 Maximum Health, +10% Critical Hit, +10 Elemental Power |
| Dive Bomber Hat | +40 Maximum Health, +15 Armor |
| Eon's Helm | +30 Maximum Health, +15 Armor, +15 Elemental Power |
| Gold Rusher Cog Cap | +9 Speed, +15 Elemental Power |
| Hot Streak Headpiece | +10 Armor, +6 Speed, +10 Elemental Power |
| Jet Stream Helmet | +7% Critical Hit, +15 Armor, +6 Speed |
| Kaos Krown | +30 Maximum Health, +15% Critical Hit, +9 Speed |
| Mags Hat | +30 Maximum Health, +15% Critical Hit, +15 Elemental Power |
| Reef Ripper Helmet | +15% Critical Hit, +15 Armor |
| Sea Shadow Hat | +10 Armor, +9 Speed, +7 Elemental Power |
| Shark Tank Topper | +20 Maximum Health, +15 Armor, +6 Speed |
| Shield Striker Helmet | +20 Maximum Health, +25 Armor |
| Sky Slicer Hat | +7 Armor, +15 Speed |
| Soda Skimmer Shower Cap | +15% Critical Hit, +10 Armor, +7 Elemental Power |
| Splatter Splasher Spires | +30 Maximum Health, +10 Armor, +6 Speed |
| Stealth Stinger Beanie | +15% Critical Hit, +15 Elemental Power |
| Sun Runner Spikes | +10% Critical Hit, +10 Armor, +10 Elemental Power |
| Thump Trucker Hat | +60 Maximum Health, +7 Armor |
| Tomb Buggy Skullcap | +25% Critical Hit, +7 Armor |

# Legendary Treasures

You'll find Legendary Treasures inside the Epic Treasure Chests you gather in each level. Some of these treasures have special bonus abilities, while others are just for kicks. Try to find them all!

- Beach Ball
- Bioluminescent Mushroom
- Black Hole
- Blue Goal
- Boom Box
- Chompy Ball
- Elemental Flower Pot
- Elemental Gem
- Elemental Torch
- Eon Statue
- Food Stand
- Kaos Punching Bag
- Live Wire Lock
- Red Goal
- Sheep Ball
- Shrink Ray
- Snap Shot Doll
- Spitfire Doll
- SuperChargers Rug
- Toy Boat Racetrack
- Toy Car Racetrack
- Toy Plane Racetrack
- Trampoline
- Traptanium Crystal
- Tree Rex Doll
- Trigger Happy Doll
- Wash Buckler Doll
- Water Fountain
- Zen Rake

## TRAINING DUMMIES

Practice your moves on these dummies—if you hit them just right, you'll get a shower of coins!

- Anvil Rain
- Battle Hammer
- Darklight Crypt
- Dragon's Peak
- Empire of Ice
- Fiery Forge
- Healing Elixir
- Hidden Treasure
- Piggy Bank
- Midnight Museum
- Mirror of Mystery
- Platinum Sheep
- Sheep Wreck Island
- Sky Diamond
- Sky-Iron Shield
- Sunscraper Spire
- Tike Speaky
- Tower of Time

# Magic Items

There are a few types of Magic Items you can interact with at Skylanders Academy. Take a look!

## COIN DISPENSERS

No need to attack these guys—they'll give you coins just for interacting with them.

- Arkeyan Crossbow
- Dragonfire Cannon
- Ghost Pirate Swords
- Hand of Fate
- Rocket Ram
- Scorpion Striker Catapult

## SPEED BOOSTERS

Get around the Academy quicker with these items.

- Time Twister Hourglass
- Winged Boots

## OTHER MAGIC ITEMS

You'll have to try these for yourself to see how they work!

- Groove Machine
- Nightmare Express
- Pirate Ship
- Sparx the Dragonfly
- Volcanic Vault

73

# RACING

Whether it's on Land, Sea, or Sky, the Skylanders SuperChargers are ready to race! Racing Mode puts your driving skills to the test with a variety of courses in a myriad of fantastic locations. Warm up during a Single Race then compete against yourself in a Time Trial. Ah, but that's not all! Once you've sharpened your abilities, take a ride on one of the high-octane Elemental racetracks to see how you really measure up. Navigate the treacherous Land environment, take a dive into the Sea, and soar through the Sky to victory.

Say hello to Pandergast at Skylanders Academy to begin your journey. You'll be a master motorist in no time!

## Racing Power-Ups

Pick up these items along the track to give your driver an edge over the competition—or the clock!

### TIKI SPEAKY
Destroy your enemies with a lightning strike!

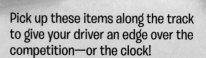

**HEALING ELIXIR**
Restore your power with a simple swig!

### SKY-IRON SHIELD
Use this to protect yourself from damage.

**GROOVE MACHINE**
Gain speed and invulnerability in a flash!

### POWERED PODS
Grab one of these so you can fire your vehicle's weapons without losing any energy. They only work for a short period of time.

**TIME TWISTER HOURGLASS**
Bring your enemies to a crawl by slowing down time.

**WINGED BOOTS**
Take off with a boost of speed!

### ROCKET RAM
Turn into an invulnerable, high-speed machine.

# RACING ON LAND: DRIFTING

When racing a Land Vehicle, make sure you know when to use your brakes, when to reverse, and when to drift. Learning how to drift will give you the quick speed boost you need to win.

## Chompy Garden

**Who wouldn't want to go for a drive through a lush green garden full of vicious little Chompies?** This three-lap race is pretty straightforward, and the course doesn't have many sharp turns. That doesn't mean it's easy, though! Watch out for puddles in the Chompy Garden, and steer clear of bursting vines and magnified sunbeams. Take advantage of the boost pads, and you'll do fine!

## Dragon Spine

**Oh, why can't these two dragons just get along?** This tight-turning course is home to two dangerous dragons. The red one breathes fire, while the blue one breathes icy patches all over the track. Fortunately, you can take advantage of them in some places by driving your vehicle right up a dragon's back. Good luck!

# RACING AT SEA: DIVING

There's nothing like a refreshing dip in the Sea! These courses mostly take place above water, but you'll need to know how to dive beneath the tides in order to forge ahead. Be patient as you learn to navigate the choppy ocean waves.

## Frozen Fossil Festival

**It may look like a cozy winter wonderland, but this icy terrain makes for some difficult driving.** This track isn't a loop, so it won't help to memorize all the turns after the first lap! Keep an eye out for tunnels in the icebergs as you make your way through the course. You'll also need to decide whether you want to drive around hunks of ice or dive below them with your seafaring ship!

## Mystical Vault

**It'll take more than speed and strength to get through the Mystical Vault!** When you hear a sneezing sound, that means the boost gates are about to change color. If you drive on the wrong color, you'll get stuck and lose lots of time! Time your race just right and avoid dangerous detours to make the grade on this tricky racetrack.

# RACING IN THE SKY: BARREL ROLL

The Sky Vehicles fly high among the clouds! Be careful, though, they can't quite come to a complete stop. Use a barrel roll to make sharp turns when you're in a jam.

## Calamity Canyon

**Uh-oh! There's a massive food fight happening all around Calamity Canyon, which is going to make it difficult for you to see out of your vehicle.** In case that's not chaotic enough for you, you'll also have to deal with flying pirates, hanging clotheslines and pennants, and boarded-up boost gates. See why they call it Calamity Canyon?

## Cloud Factory

**The Cloud Factory's track is deceptively simple—just one big loop.** But once you get going, you'll find that the steep climbs and sharp drops can disorient even the most skilled fliers. This course is filled with dangerous purple tornadoes and lightning storms, too. Stay safe!

# EXTRA QUESTS

Tessa, Buzz, and Hugo are waiting at Skylanders Academy to give extra quests to ambitious Portal Masters.

## QUESTS FROM TESSA

**Once you complete the chapters in Monstrous Isles, keep an eye out for Tessa.** She'll be offering up brand-new quests right outside the Academy. Not all of these very special missions are available at first. You'll have to unlock them as you go. After completing three quests, you must wait a day before Tessa offers additional quests.

**Hugo reveals three new quests every day, but only after you've made it through the Bandit Train.** Not all the quests are available immediately, but go say hello to Hugo, anyway; he's also hanging out by the Academy.

## HUGO'S DAILY QUESTS

Once you're ready to take on his quests, you can replay levels to reach every milestone! He also rewards you for completing Elemental Gate quests, winning races, and playing Skystones Overdrive. Not bad!

## BUZZ'S DRIVER

**Buzz loves to push new Skylanders to be their best.** Each SuperCharger has three driving quests—one that uses each Skylander's unique attacks, a second that is custom-built for his or her vehicle, and a SuperCharged Challenge that takes place on the racetrack. Talk to Buzz to find out what your Skylander needs to do to become the ultimate SuperCharger!

# ELEMENTAL GATES

Stop in and say hello to the Great Grizzo, Greeble extraordinaire. He's in charge of the Elemental Gate at Skylands Academy and can transform the gate's Element to synch with your vehicle. Stay focused, complete the ten challenges, and earn up to three shields based on your performance. Collect shields to gain additional Stardust and increase your Portal Master Rank.

**Air Gate:** Destroy forty enemies as fast as possible. Watch out for turrets!

**Earth Gate:** Collect twelve boulders by rolling them to the intakes.

**Tech Gate:** Catch five Sheep Thieves and return the sheep to safety.

**Fire Gate:** Reach the goal. Try to avoid lava—it slows you down!

**Water Gate:** Escort the Scuba Sheep to the end of the shipwreck.

**Magic Gate:** Rescue twelve Mabu from their glowing bubble traps.

**Life Gate:** Save twelve Twitterpillars from spiderwebs and return them to safety.

**Undead Gate:** Find and exterminate fifty-five bugs that live under the tombstones.

**Light Gate:** Find and destroy Kaos's hidden forces in an asteroid field.

**Dark Gate:** Rescue five Scuba Sheep while fighting a nasty eel.